HERE

COMES

THIS

DREAMER

Poetry By Micah Bournes

SIDESHOW
MEDIA GROUP

8033 SUNSET BLVD. #164   LOS ANGELES, CA. 90046
sideshowmediagroup.com

SSMG PRESS / LOS ANGELES

HERE COMES THIS DREAMER
MICAH BOURNES

SSMG PRESS
COPYRIGHT ©2020

SIDESHOW MEDIA GROUP
8033 SUNSET BLVD. #164
LOS ANGELES, CA. 90046
USA
SIDESHOWMEDIAGROUP.COM

For little black kids with big black dreams

Shout out to Keayva Mitchell, Alyssa Matuchniak, and Ra Avis for your critical eyes and encouraging words. Shout out to John Bucher and Sideshow Media Group for your confidence in my writing and patience with my process.

About The Cover

Navigating America as a black man has been the strongest influence and most common theme in my writing. When I considered the cover of my first collection of poetry, it was important to collaborate with an artist who shared that experience. Austin Uzor does with paint, canvas, and visual image what I do with word, page, and metaphor.

The cover features a man of African descent at an intersection in any given city in America. America, the land of opportunity. Endless possibility for anyone willing to work hard. That is what the black man is told. Given the orientation of the subject, the green light indicates it is safe to cross, to move forward. But upon closer examination, you may notice there are greens lights in both directions, a set up, a guaranteed disaster. The invitation to proceed and participate in the hustle and bustle of western society is a trap for the black man. We cannot walk down any street safely. How then, do we move? Where then, do we belong if our home is not our home, and the land of our ancestors is so far removed?

When our reality appears impossible, we have no choice but to dream. Every step requires creativity and courage. Austin's green light intersection is a poem in itself. It perfectly captures so much of what I am hoping to communicate in this book before you even read a single poem.

Third Grade Dream

In the future I want to get a scholarship and be a pro football, soccerball, basketball, baseball player, an artist, a saxophone player, and a drummer. I want to get married to a beautiful, Christian girl whose name starts with an "M" and is from the Bible. I also want to have 4 kids, 2 boys and 2 girls. And I want to name them Matthew, Mark, Mary, and Martha. They are all names from the Bible, and they all start with an "M". We would be the M&M family. I also want to be a missionary and tell people about God.

– Micah (8 Years Old)

Micah Bournes

TABLE OF CONTENTS

NIGHTMARES

DAYDREAMS

PROPHESIES

Micah Bournes

NIGHTMARES

The Gifted Program

Woulda been a straight A student
in the slow class
But I tested out of a chance to shine
Upgraded my proper place to
the back of a fancy bus
Elementary called it G.A.T.E.
Junior high T.A.P.
Never knew what them letters stood for
It didn't matter
All it meant was more homework
That was no gift

Before we could color inside the lines
the state of California
gerrymandered our playground
Creating a   class
                  system

of   gifted   —   gifted-nots
Prophesying which children would become
         doctors   Which felons
Deciding who deserved
         investment   Who was
                                    human-waste
                                    of time

The gifted program segregated
         the supreme youth...
         and me
from   the unremarkable
From   the kids who bore my image

As a black boy in a sea of pale genius
I knew this responsibility was 400 years heavy
I spent K through 8
proving I deserved to remain
somewhere I never wished to be
Chained to someone else's dream

Plucked out of   the village
                                        that raised this exceptional
        child
Stumbling through advanced courses
with a mind
stronger than   poverty
weaker than
        privilege
I had risen from
                                        the depths
Desperately treading water

Fat lips
poking out
just above the waves

Inner-City Boys Asking Questions
On A Hike At Summer Camp
In The Mountains At Night

Yooooooooooo
oooooooooooo
oooooooooooo
oooooooooooo

You mean to tell me
all them stars
been right up there
in that same sky
this whole time?

        How come we can't
        see 'em back in Long Beach?

    What?
    What does light pollution mean?
        How can light pollute anything?
        How can light make
        somethin' harder to see?

      DID Y'ALL HEAR THAT NOISE?
    What noise...?
    Oh
    Snap
        THAT noise
    What was that?
        Is that a deer?
    A bear?
A lion?
    Foo' there ain't no lions up here
    Does this look like Africa to you?
Oh yeah?
You ever heard of
a MOUNTAIN lion?

Oh
Snap
Was that a lion?
            How come this white boy
            over here cryin'?
            Y'all see this white boy cryin'?
Oh you mean homie that
was tryna act hard?
      What he say?
            Say he wanna go home?
            Is y'all tryna go home?
            I ain't tryna go home
            It's tight up here right?
                  How come we gotta
                  go home at all?
                  How come we can't stay here?
With the swimming pool
and the lake
and the canoes
      And all this food
            And no whoopins
                  And   all   these   stars?
                  How come we don't get no stars
                  back in Long Beach?
Oh yeah
      What does light pollution mean?
                  How come our chests be burnin'
                  if the air up here s'pose to be clean?

            Why is it harder to breathe
            the closer we get to God?
                  How can light pollute anything?

Micah Bournes

How come we gotta
go home at all?
How come God made **us** live
where there ain't no stars?

Manna

Yesterday me and Momma drove past
what used to be McDonald's
One with a plastic-tube playground and ball pit
A poor kid's Disneyland
It was outer space
It was heaven
It was somewhere I always hoped to go
The golden arches had disappeared
The pearly gates fell off the hinges
Windows covered with plywood
No children at play
I reminisced

Remember when dem burgers
cost 29 cent on Tuesdays?

YES
Momma worshipped
GOD DID IT
JUST FOR ME

Offering praise for the way
she could feed 6 kids and herself
with 2 dollars and some change

God did it—
God created McDonald's
With that microwaved test-tube meat
Made it cheap so the babies could eat
To hell with anyone who says fast food
shouldn't accept EBT
Mickey D's is why I'm alive
You can't get one leaf of lettuce for 29 cents

Micah Bournes

God did it—
Just for me—
Just for my Momma—

And it broke my heart to know
we was so po'
poison tasted like a miracle
Manna from heaven

Thirsty souls drink dirty water
with gratitude
Hungry hearts eat crumbs
that fall from tables of the rich

Call it grace
And I can't decide if I should shake
my fist at the heavens
or second Momma's praise wit' an amen

King Of The Concrete Jungle

Mean muggin' is a mask
melted into my skin
I lied for so long

I forgot where
I hid the boy
I was protecting

I never wanted to be mean
Just alive
Just respected

Being gentle and
innocent never saved
black boys

from being brutalized
I transformed into the stereotype
hoping to scare the real dangers away

I *will* steal
and murder
and rape

your everything
Please stay far
far away from this beast

If I must be killed
as something
less than man

Christ
I'll be hunted as lion
before slaughtered as lamb

The Ghost Of Detroit

My father's father was
dead for days before
anyone noticed

No missing persons report
No unanswered phone calls
No concerned or nosy neighbors

While delivering nothing
besides coupons and advertisements
I wonder if the mailman inhaled

the corpse screaming
for the promised earth
I don't recall the way

his body was discovered
I only remember
he died alone

in the comfort
or prison of his self-made
isolation:

an introvert's perfect exit—
or perhaps a grump who died friendless
I only met the man once— (once was enough)

Upon hearing of his death
I blinked and blinked but
could not cure the dryness

My father flew alone to visit
the ghost of Detroit
Before he left

and when he returned
I never saw him cry
I never asked if

he loved his father
But I do wonder:
Were his tears dammed up

by masculine tradition?
Or had masculine tradition
made a desert of three generations?

My Government Name

MICAH

The humble prophet of
justice and mercy

The faith
of my parents

The infamous me everyone
thinks they know

KEITA

The royal African dynasty

The broken chains of
my uncle's revolution

The truest me no one
ever calls for

BOURNES

The noose tying me to a
European family tree I'll never
be grafted into

The deception of supremacy
and patriarchy
disguised as tradition and love

The gift from my father
One that I hate
but cannot bring myself
to destroy

"They might think they've got a pretty good jump shot, or a pretty good flow, but our kids can't all aspire to be LeBron or Lil' Wayne. I want them aspiring to be scientists and engineers, doctors and teachers, not just ballers and rappers. I want them aspiring to be a Supreme Court Justice. I want them aspiring to be the President of the United States of America." – President Barack Obama

Hoopers And MCs

There are far more
black rappers and NBA players
than presidents and astronauts

but no one applauds our dreams
Black boys wanting to be
hoopers and MCs
are ignorant ghetto babies

Our teachers claimed we could become
whatever we want
As long as we wanted
what they wanted us to want
As long as our desires were patriotic
or reasonable

Reasonable
like the way they encourage kids who
set their sights on The Oval Office
or the moon
then scold black boys on the
slim chance of gettin' signed
or goin' pro

You ain't protectin' our naïve minds
You scared of gettin' dunked on
You scared of your grandkids gyratin'

to the soundtrack of our rebellion
Since when has this pipeline to prison
cared about the future of black boys?

Don't murder our imaginations in
the name of being realistic
Realistic dreams are oxymorons
Realistic dreams are nothin' but
a list of errands to run before death
You ain't savin' us from nothin'

If we fail
If
we fail

wisdom gained from our
hard-earned defeat will
fertilize the next defiant dream
we decide to spring from
this blood-rich soil

Failure
is not a dream-killer
It's a rite of passage
A wack mixtape
is a black boy's bar mitzvah
It's how I became a man

A reminder to
keep rappin' even when
the whole world denies
my dopeness
My humanity

Whatchu know about bein' told
you garbage
and still believin' you

the greatest rapper alive?
Whatchu know about bein' told
you devilish
and still believin'
you carry the image of God?
We have mastered the ceremony
of self-celebration

So what if all black boys got the same dreams?
So what if we all aim to be
poets over beats and
gravity-defying champions?

Such a poetic justice
if the only contribution black men make
to American society is
somethin' to dance to
and broken ankles

So what if we never make it?
So what if we never go platinum?
So what if we never get drafted?
So what if we never get treated with
justice and equality?

Of course America wants us to believe
that some things are so unlikely to happen
it's a waste of time to even have a dream

But

I have a dream
I have a dream
I have a dream

Micah Bournes

Where It Counts

With a smile and a wink
the white lady claimed
her white husband was black

where it counts

This was her activism
Her solidarity

I wrapped my waist in glory
Angels guarding Eden
from its former masters

May Eve never again
pluck the strange fruit
Sink her fangs into the cock

I bet she's kinky
Whipping her groom's pale back
Screaming for his nigger-dick
to rape her harder

She believes in change and hope
She voted for Obama
She'd blow him too
Everyone has room to grow
but she stands up

where it counts

I breathe steady
Inhale her violence
I cannot afford a war today
My mind is a calm blue sky
Not a white cloud in sight

Some days I must turn my back
on this world to survive it
Some days
I must live in my dreams
if I want to be anything
more than rage

There Goes The Neighborhood

Babe's Kitchen is one of those classic diners
frozen in nostalgia
It feels like black and white television
It feels like a time before my time
yet somehow too familiar
All of the employees are related
All of the employees are senior citizens
A *real American-family-business*
A pillar of the community
feeding the blue collars of Long Beach
long before Snoop Dogg
Long before the city *changed*

Somebody's grandfather came to take our order
He looked me up and down and asked

Did you register when you moved into the
neighborhood?

I couldn't decide
if he was a cold racist
asking a racist question
or a friendly racist
telling a racist joke

Either way
I was not amused

But I laughed

As the awkward chuckle passed through my lips
it tasted like The Eucharist
Like blood in my mouth

My stomach churned as I imagined it would if I ate human
flesh

I felt like Judas
Like Christ
Betraying myself then
hanging in silence as I'm crucified

I wanted to prove him wrong

I wanted to stand up and list off my credentials
in words with more syllables than his simple mind could take

                I wanted to prove him right

    I wanted to stand up and fire off hyphenated profanities
        Inventing new conjugations for four letter words
          like the dumbest nigga he done eva heard

I wanted to prove him wrong

I wanted to leave and come back with the black elite
A fleet of the sharpest
darkest
intellectuals he's ever seen
Leaving tips large enough to buy out this business twice over

                I wanted to prove him right

        I wanted to leave and come back
            with thugs and hoodrats
            with chains guns and bats
              burn this place to ash

But what did I do?
I laughed

Then sat there silently
Then ran home and wrote poetry?
Then SCREAMED it out like I'm not a coward?
Like I didn't cry in front of my computer screen?
Like I wasn't waiting for my two white friends to speak up for me?
Like I stood up for myself?
Like I did SOMETHING?
Like I fought a revolution?
Like IT WASN'T FUNNY
Like I didn't laugh

But I did

And it tasted like The Eucharist

Like blood in my mouth

and I swallowed it

Native Tongue

According to ShakespeareOnline.Com, The English language owes a great debt to Shakespeare. He invented over seventeen hundred of our common words by changing nouns into verbs, changing verbs into adjectives, connecting words never before used together, adding prefixes and suffixes, and devising words wholly original.

If I could
I'd spit this in whateva'
mother tongue was

        ripped

          from

            our

              mothers'

                lips

But the closest I got to that

Is hip hop
    Is black talk
Is improper
    Nonproper
Unproper
    Uneducated
Un-dash-educated
    Un-scratch-assimilated
Me talk
    We talk
Our talk
    Make y'all wish y'all knawmtalmbout talk
Make y'all ask ya black friend talk
    Make y'all run to urban dictionary dot com talk
That ONE thing
    That SOMETHING that belongs to **us**
That **us** you try to demonize

Envy
Copy
Despise
That **us** you try to categorize
Stereotype
Try to shame our broken English you wish you could understand
But you can't neva get it because
We stay fly
We stay fresh
We stay change
We stay every day new way to say we neva believed your lies
We neva spoke your tongue
We BEEN ineducated
Uneducated
Un-dash-educated
Un-SCRATCH-assimilated
And if your EVA
wanna know what we talmbout
maybe you need to unlearn a thing or two
Who says our vernacular ain't classical?
Who says rap lyricists are anything less than Shakespearean?

Shakespeare: a man who turned nouns into verbs and "invented" seventeen hundred words

That's funny
When we break the rules
we're called ignorant
When we "invent" words
they're called slang
The way we talk is

Improper
       Nonproper
Unproper
       Uneducated
Un-dash-educated
       Un-scratch-assimilated

WE AIN'T NEVA BEEN DUMB

We break
      Eng-
   lish
      like chains

This *is* our native tongue

Glass Dollars

Boooooooy was them white folks clappin'

Wasn't worth the loot

Nowadays I'm rubbin' two nickels
tryna break into the chitlin circuit
But I ain't nothin' special over here
Ain't that a blessin'

I was never good as them white folks
thought I was
Had me thinkin' I was walkin' on water
'steada tap dancin' on glass dollars

Till one day
my black boot
landed on that stage
with a flatfoot truth
A big-boneded joy

Fell straight through the platform

Remembered who I was
Remembered who I'll never be
No matter how loud the

roarin'
chompin'
applause

No Common Ground

Death row inmates receive their favorite supper
before the empire gently injects them with death
Oh how generous the hands that play
the hand of God
May we all die hungry
May we never legitimize the lies they name mercy
The privileged sing of unity
Their false hymn falls on ears deafened by
the sound of death
Gunshots crack the air like whips
Men in uniform afraid of weaponless boys
Black boys with smiles that float like ghosts in the night
The cowards shoot first then cry for peace in the street
We cannot hear your pleas over our own life-mourning wails
The land is divided by rivers of our blood
There is no middle ground to stand on
Do you supreme ones not remember?
Your decrees proclaimed us devils
Demons must not compromise with gods
It is our nature to rebel
Crash the gates of a heaven
free from our darkness
Spill midnight rebellion onto white-robed dreams
Drag you deities back to earth
Teach you to unworship yourselves
Name you brother again
There is no peace to be made
as long as you remain above us
Our blood has made this profane land holy
We will never search for common ground

Will The World Be Fixed By A Hipster Government?

"One day our generation is gonna rule the population, so we keep on waiting, waiting, waiting on the world to change." – John Mayer

My math may be off
but weren't these the hippies at Woodstock?
The pot-smoking lovers of peace?
The ones who raged against the machine they now operate?

Well

They *did* legalize weed

But still

Win Or Lose

Half the nation will be mourning
Win or lose
there is no cause for champagne
The fall of the wicked
does not resurrect
the caged skeleton of a child
Does not rapture destruction
back into the drone's belly
Does not change
the hearts of a people
who hate themselves in half
Who delight in an enemy's disgrace
Win or lose
America is America
We can only dance like slaves
No one deserves a parade

Fallen Titans
For Liam Neeson

A fictional messiah who saves the world in every film says
—Hollywood sexual allegations against men have become *a bit
of a witch hunt*—

But everyone knows
witches don't have penises
Everyone knows
witches don't have earthly power

Witches aren't protected by the law
By their influential friends
By a culture that believes they're generally good people
despite their generally bad everything

Witches have never been kings to be dethroned
Witches are always the scapegoat of kings
The ones slaughtered on the altars of men
Blamed for every man's sin until all men are innocent again

Everyone knows only men are holy
Everyone knows priests don't have vaginas
Everyone knows witches don't have penises
My friend

These fallen titans are too godly to be witches
This is not a witch hunt
These are witches
refusing to be hunted

anymore

Boomin'

The windshield has a spider-web crack
  The brakes screech a prehistoric caw
    The key will not open the driver's side door
      The insurance check from the accident was used to pay rent
       The hood and left fender remain dented
        The bucket is busted enough to not bother fixin'
         But dem speakers doe
          The first thing I did was replace the
          stock system with something so ign'ant the
         seats became massage chairs
        I need to feel the beauty boomin' through my body
       I listen to hip hop with my entire being
      I listen to hip hop with my tense neck
    My knotted back
  My aching feet
   My bloody guts
     It chops and hits and pushes and gives
       voice to this blackness
         Bittersweet like the hands of the masseuse
          Somewhere between gratitude and
           this hurts a lot more than I imagined
            All I want is health
            Not luxury
           All I need is a beat that knocks the defeat
          from my shoulders
        Makes me stand up straight
       No tranquilizing lullabies
     No rose-tinted anthems
   No gentle rub
    No pat on the back
      I wanna feel the weight
        like barefoot children
          dancin' up and down my spine

Gang Gang

We stank-faced our way into family
Strangers became home over
questionable mac-n-cheese
We uptown boujee 'bout our
downhome country food
Cacklin' at unspoken thoughts
We hurdled over nice-to-meet-yous
Went straight to

Can't take y'all nowhere
but please don't leave me 'lone
in a room like this

We gang gang forever
before we even knew names
We eye-rollers
shade-thrower
Sound-system hijackers
Next thing I know
two of us choreographed-steppin' to Outkast
We will never be the turkey
at a pilgrim's feast
If we dance
it's for the good of our own feet

We keep strollin' in late 'till
the room fills with so much blackness I'm
embarrassed for having shown up on time
We mingle to survive
until a room-cutting glance erupts
all the codes switching in our throats
We toss our heads back and
billow black happiness thicker
than small chatter
Our laughter floats into envious nostrils

Everyone chokes on
our volcanic joy

Micah Bournes

And So I Didn't Tell José He Was A Good Father

And then my daughter decides to have
an autistic breakdown
and this older Mexican lady just keeps
lookin' at me
Shakin' her head like

> This ain't nothin' a
> good whoopin' can't fix

But I'm not about to explain myself
to this lady
> Oh no Ma'am
> It's not what you think
> My daughter has a condition

It ain't none of her business
She don't even know me

And my friends try to be nice like
> Oh José
> You're a single dad
> That's so hard
> You're doin' such a great job

But how do they know?
My daughter doesn't even talk
unless my ex wife comes around
Why won't she talk to me?

And I got all these tattoos
back in the day
And I thought about it like
I was collecting art or somethin'
you know

But this neighborhood is crazy
All these dudes keep
askin' me where I'm from
And I'm like
      I got a kid bro
      85% custody
      I ain't about none of that

And I love my tattoos
I don't regret it or nothin'
but sometimes
I kinda regret it
you know

And I just wish I could tell
someone all of this without
them tellin' me
I'm doin' a good job
How could they know?
I don't even know
I think about that all the time

Am I being a good dad?
I just wish I could have that
direct line to heaven like

      God

      God

      Am I being a good father?

Micah Bournes

Gringo Salsa

This salsa was crafted for gringo tongues
yet the natural R rollers might also enjoy
the tropical
savory blend
Nectarous pineapple
Onion and cilantro
Ripe tomato
Gentle spice

To hungry souls in poisoned barrios
Where even a cool drink of water burns hot with lead
Do not deem yourself a traitor when entering a Trader Joe's
One that replaced a childhood memory
Do not scold yourself for buying the pineapple salsa

and enjoying it

You have swallowed fire for far too many years
Never believe you are not an authentic expression of
your heritage unless you enjoy the scorching
Never let anyone convince you
that being proud of your pain
is the same as being proud of your people

Your people are not only habanero bold
They are sweet as mangoes
This gringo salsa is still salsa
Of course things stolen from your culture
might remind you of home

Grandma's Yes

I didn't know what segregation was
'till I left Mississippi
We didn't call it no segregation
We didn't call it nothin' at all
Black folks was just s'pose live here
Shop there
Go to church down the way
But we ain't have no place to go to school

Our principal started
Prentiss Institute underneath
a big ol' oak tree
So thick even when it rained
wouldn't nothin' come through

He taught us a different kind of respect
Said that we was students
Not soldiers
Not slaves
We don't say
Yes Sir No Sir
We don't say
Yes Ma'am No Ma'am
We let our yes be yes
and our no be no
Just like the good Lord said

Then one day I walked into a store
The white lady behind the counter said
        Can I help you?
And I said
        Yes

That woman looked at me like
I cursed her god

She said
    Caaaaan I help you?
And I said
    Yeeeees

Lament For Mother Tubman

The median net worth for non-immigrant African-American households in the Greater Boston region is $8. The household median net worth was $247,500 for whites.

> — The Color of Wealth in Boston:
> A 2015 report by the Federal
> Reserve Bank of Boston,
> Duke University, and the New School.

America promises to print Harriet Tubman
on a twenty-dollar bill
A cruel and unusual honor
Let the faces of greed remain on their god
Give Caesar what belongs to Caesar
but keep my Momma out yo' filthy palms

Remember all the nothing that changed
when this nation literally tokenized
Sacagawea in fake gold
Remember how indigenous people
still live in squalor

You can't blackface a dollar
and call it reparations
Newly bred Tubmans
crammed into privileged wallets
Sardined in bank vaults like
the hulls of slave ships
Businessmen pass a pimp
a stack of Harriets to rape
a teenage sex slave with African hips
While Mother Tubman's
daughters and sons struggle
to keep the heat on

In Boston
a black father dies
after decades of wanting to
New England's bitterness
finally froze his will to hope
He left his family a modest inheritance:
a suicide-note-apology
8 dollars
and a special edition Celtics Jersey

In Boston
a black mother dies
after decades of refusing to
After freedom marches and protests
After cancer stole both breasts
After spending her savings
on saving herself
She leaves her daughter
a closet full of church hats
an award-winning
corn bread recipe
and a family Bible with
8 dollars hidden in
Philippians 4:19
My God will supply every need

America really believes they doin' us a favor
Painting our faces on their dreams
Writing "In God We Trust"
on this blasphemous economy
Assigning net worth to human beings

Life ought to be priceless
but only the breath of the
highly appraised gets protected
No wonder this nation considered us

Micah Bournes

more useful as slaves
Capitalism ascribes
an 8 dollar value to free black lives
If Mother Tubman were alive today
she would need two and a half selves
before she was worth the weight
of her very own bill

2020

5 years beyond Back To The Future's future
8 years beyond the Mayan apocalypse
2 decades beyond Y2K
We exist in a future we worried
would never be

I exist in a history I worry
will never die

My white friend
cries
Ashamed of her naivety
Not realizing her father was
more than a socially acceptable
amount of racist
Said he was disgusted
at the thought of her holding
her new Kenyan boyfriend's hand

I thought of the hugs we've shared
Of how repulsed he would be
by our gentleness
I thought of King's dream
Still a dream
I thought of Langston's dream
Still deferred
I wondered how short
the fuse must be by now

I thought of Frederick Douglass
Of his marriage
to a white woman
in the 1800's
shortly after his first
and black wife
stopped dreaming forever

Micah Bournes

I thought of dreams
I thought of future
Of how it will disappoint me
Of how it is 2020 and we still
don't have flying cars
or hoverboards

I thought of time
Of how it will not save my children
I thought of love
Of how it always takes courage
no matter what century
it is beaten
and burning
and dreaming in

The Exceptional Smiles of Nina and Jimmy

Their skulls rested
gently against each other
Touching at the temple of their minds
Their smiles seemed impossible
How could such joy could exist
back then (even for a moment)
in bodies
so black
so sugar in the tank
so full of rage

Their taste—
Deep fried caviar
Backporch blues and Johann Sebastian Bach
"Now is the winter of our discontent" 'cause
"Life ain't been no crystal stair"

But they kept climbing
Exceptional indeed
Unfit for every community
they loved

There they were
Chasin' the devil
away with those grins

At first I wondered what
revelation must have grown
from such brilliance in discourse

But most likely
Nina and Jimmy were
arguing over whether or not grits
should have remained in the slave days
James called them things

Micah Bournes

"pale
lumpy
tasteless porridge"
Something that oughta be
"served as a punishment for sins"

After the third glass of wine
they were surely comparing the girth
of their lovers' egos
Trading stories
until coughing seized their gravel throats

It is hard to tell the difference
between choking and laughing
when you have swallowed so much smoke
When you have escaped a burning home
time and time again

What is the difference between a lucky nigger
and a cursed one?
Either way
all your friends are dead or poor
There is no comfort in being the exception
But there is jubilee in finding another

DAYDREAMS

Milo Jackson

My friends waited three days
to name their child

I wrote an entire book
without a title

People ask about my dreams
I do not trust their curiosity

I tell them I have none
as they stretch and swell inside

I must hold them before
I name them

If I ever introduce you to them
your opinions will be useless

They are here already
Living

Growing
Answer to no other reality

Tenda Headed

Most us boys is tenda headed
Black girls been yanked at the root
since before they can remember
They already know how much the magic costs
    First time Momma gave me braids
    I seen the face of Jesus
    I twitched and screamed like that kitchen table
    was Guantanamo bay
        Boy sit still
        Boy you already got so much hair
        Just watch
        This'll make it grow even more
    I ain't never checked the science of that
    But all black folks I known believe it
    I had dreams of afro tall as
    white girls hair be long
So every two weeks I sat through torture
Let Momma or big sista' twist my natural into corn-rows
crop-circles zig-zags triangles loopty-loops
Whereva their heavy-handed spirit would lead
    After while I squirmed less and less and less
    Then one day
    it didn't hurt no more at all
    Matta fact it felt good
        Hands of black prophetess pullin'
        the stress right out my head
        Soothin' my soul
        Makin' me prettier with every touch
    For hours we'd talk and talk and talk
    I confessed a bunch of
    things I didn't plan on tellin' Momma
    I asked a bunch of questions I never knew

only my sister could answer
Things I would never mention in a
gut bustin' chest beatin' barber shop
Things they wouldn't know what to do wit' anyway
  Most us boys is tenda headed
  This kind'a pain
  This kind'a comfort
  Our mind too soft
This mind need a woman's touch
Momma grabbed me by the roots
Yanked 'em hard as she knew how

They grew

Iron Softens Iron
For D.J. Efechto

Your newborn death floated
still and loud in my closet
A ghost with flesh
I statued upon
the discovery
The borrowed hoodie I
meant to return

Of course you found
a way to keep me warm far
beyond your final winter
Your scent hung heavy
in its threads
I cradled the infant
ghost to my bosom

Buried my nose in its cotton skin
Swallowed echoes of a gentle man
Then statued again
Terrified and excited
by what I had done
Terrified and excited
by how soft I have become

Choppin' And Stickin'

Four black folks look around and see they're the only non-Chinese people in a Chinese restaurant in a Chinese neighborhood. It's kinda nice being a minority to a minority for a change. If we're honest, we got more in common with white folks than Chinese immigrants, but somethin' about this situation feels comfortable. Like Mama Lu's Dumpling house might really be Mama Lu's Soul Food Kitchen. The waiter was uncommonly hospitable. Or maybe, it's just, he didn't treat us like we were black in America. He treated us like guests in his home. Out of courtesy he asked if we'd be okay with chopsticks or if we needed forks. *Oh, you think because we black we don't know how to use chopsticks?* We needed forks. *I needed a fork.* But we stuck with chopsticks, and that Chinese brotha smiled real big. The food came and we got to choppin' and stickin' and talkin' and reminiscin' and laughin' way too loud and telling each other to quiet down. We didn't wanna appear to be *too different.* We didn't wanna draw too much attention. As long as we stayed quiet and used these difficult utensils and minded our own business we'd blend right in! But no matter how hard we tried, we were all something different. And that difference was different even from each other. Between the four of us, we spanned the whole spectrum of blackness. Rappers and Ivy League graduates. Bible college and masters degrees, engineers, entrepreneurs, beer brewers, event planners, black Greeks, debutants, all the way to "why fancy restaurants give you three forks," and "do y'all really know how to use these chopsticks?" We made a covenant that we would not judge each other by how much meat was left on our chicken bones, but by the content of our character. We agreed that our blackness was not a competition or a curse. Not to be hidden or put on display. We reminded ourselves that it is okay to be different. That no matter how many times we are treated with contempt, we will never apologize for existence. We made a covenant that we will never accept a world like our nation. We will never accept a nation like our nation. Because in this tiny corner of America, we were able to be ourselves freely without being treated like black people in America. We were treated like guests in a good man's home. Like immigrants in a nation of immigrants. Like we're so clearly different, and that's what makes us exactly like our uncommonly kind Chinese host. *"Excuse me brotha, can I get a fork though?"*

Micah Bournes

Depraved Inheritance

Her spoon would shovel through
mountains of buttery ice cream
Mining out the pecans

I never understood
why Momma wouldn't just
buy a jar of nuts

Countless times I opened the tub
to discover the milky soil
pillaged of its treasure

I swore on all things holy
I would never commit
such an abomination

Lord be merciful
Evil came upon me
this dawn

Spoon in hand
I defiled my roommate's ice cream
Unearthing nuggets of cookie dough

as songbirds
were drowned out
by the rooster's mocking crow

Suddenly I remembered
Then laughed myself to tears
at my depraved inheritance

Whiskey Love

The unspoken tension
was finally unfelt
Call it maturity
Forgiveness
A perspective shift
from half empty
to whiskey love
So potent there's no need
to brim the glass

Swirl it gentle
Let it breathe

Family is a powerful elixir
Don't guzzle
what is meant to be sipped
then blame the substance
for being too strong
There is wisdom in limits

May this lineage
never again chug obligation
down our throats
Shame ourselves
into vulnerable

Love is not love
if it dizzies you open
If it vomits you empty
If it hangs you over
and over

Micah Bournes

Know the difference between
holding close
and keeping captive
Abandoning
and breaking free

Never drowning in affection
Let this gene pool be a life-spring
A stiff drink
that keeps the heart warm

Coming

After Lauren Sanderson's "Leaving"

Here there are only metaphors
The sky falls desperately short
but still is the closest grandness

The birds returning for spring
The birds
The returning
The spring
All more than they seem
All some kind of messiah

Everything is beauty
but nothing is clear
So we'll stay silent
Stay listening to the song
the broad-jawed day
always sings
The face cratered on the moon
looks exactly like everyone we miss
guiding us through the night
The women who left us
never left
Never stop coming
with light

Micah Bournes

Yes. I'm Here. What Happened?

You pierced the air with my name
The wind carried its blood
I followed the trail to your feet
Dressed for a funeral
Arms full of apology
When did I become so ready to mourn?
Who convinced me that no one
can scream my name with a mouth full of joy?
Has it been that long since I was loved?
Have I ever been?

Desire is dangerous
Dreams are instruments with sharp edges
We were taught not to run with them
I do not want to hurt anyone
I am careful to no avail
A virgin full of fear

still covered in blood

I have worried myself
into an open wound
I have worried my name
into a shame-conjuring curse
What did you want again?

Nothing?

But me?

Tonight, At Least

We built a treehouse
in brittle branches
Romanced our wobbly shack with candlelight
Told silent stories with tongues and lips
Listened with our necks
Created a language of our own
An uncrackable code
yet still spoke in whispers
Giddy children
feeling loved in a house never meant to be home
Ignoring that particular sadness
Hearing the creaks in the bones of our paradise
Believing in faith
tonight
at least
these branches will not break

The Crab And The Crane

We are the paranoid crab
scurrying frantic in no particular direction
Returning to the same place
content
with nothing

but our own fears disturbing this silent
holy night
We are the crane's legs
buckling backwards
Appearing to move away yet

growing closer with each denial
We become what we name ourselves
We christened us doomed
Viewing every good thing
through apocalyptic lens

Remember how I wasn't what you expected?
Remember how your panic never arrived?
Do you wonder what would happen
if we chose to call good .   .   .

good?

If I Believed In Signs

After wondering if she might be dead
I remembered
her name was spelled
with two consecutive Rs

There she is

Breathing

Glowing

as she was
in Mrs. Peterson's 3rd grade class

Here she is
Like me
still in the city of
our childish dreams
I wonder how many coffee shops
we've sat in opposite corners
How often our shadows
must have reached and reached

The internet informs me
we've evolved into
the same kind of outcast
What luck to be handed
a regimented destiny
and fail our way into poets

If I believed in signs
this would be
another warning to ignore

Micah Bournes

All my friends are poets
All my friends say it is
foolish to love a poet
None of us have ever
listened to conventional wisdom

We bitter
and sweeten our own hearts
again and again

I wonder if she knows
what I never spoke at 8 years of age
I wonder how gentle
it will sting if she chooses not
to follow me back

I am content
I promise
I am not searching for love
But I am searching the world wide web
for a crush from 20 years ago
and I don't know why

All I know is
I have lied to myself
again and again
I promise
I am content

*She followed me back

What Could Be

I'll write a poem about
the way you dance
to the song I wrote
about the way you sing
and we'll keep inspiring each other until
we can't tell whose art is whose
Whose heart is whose
Synchronizing our beats to create a love stronger
than we ever dreamed
Our dreams will seem so silly and small as we
thank God for the wonder of our reality
And when reality seems less than wonderful
we'll stroll through the galleries we painted
to remember that it is
We'll spin our own records and hear our own voices
Listen as they sing old pains
now heard as new prophecies
Young faith asking weary saints
"Don't you still believe?"
And we will believe
again
And dance and sing
again
With bad knees
And static-filled prayers
Just enough signal to
to reach the God who's everywhere
We'll thank the Lord for the choices we made
The risk we decided to take
The time we didn't know
but knew there was
only one way to see...

Nothing I Needed

I dreamt about kissing a woman
I've wanted to kiss for a decade
      I was close once
      But God spoke her out of
      loving me
      In good faith
      she set flame to
      everything we built
      Asked to remain friends
We are kissing
in my dream
until
one by one
my teeth begin to dislodge
from my gums
I spit them out hastily
like prayer of a hungry child
required to grace his dinner

There was no blood
Only teeth
and terror on her face
I attempt to rescue the moment
Convinced we could make it work
with lips and tongue and passion
I've lost nothing I needed
My love was freed from its bite
But it was no longer welcomed

I shared the dream with her
She claimed it was confirmation
Proof we were never meant to be
Then asked for my interpretation
I thought of all the nonsensical worlds
my slumbering mind has invented

Shrugged my shoulders and said
"I ate a bunch of junk food last night"
She could not understand
my dismissal of the prophecy
I could not understand
why our God only told her no

Still I believe
I've lost nothing I needed
But everyone I've wanted
has left
with the brightness of my smile

A Simple Dream

We sleep through the alarms
because there are none
No red-flag romance
No soul-sucking office to be late to
We wake to the taste of light in the air

I love the way our small
living-space in this big city
is called a studio
To live
is to create

We fill our closet of-a-home with wide-open ideas
I rise to write when
the fog of dreams has yet to clear
You rise to draw when
the sun burns soft with blue of a newborn day

Our parents
are not proud
Never will be
Cannot understand why we
"like being poor"

We fell in love again when
we stopped trying to explain
—Disapproval
does not destroy us
the way it once did—

We nearly shipwrecked
our simple dream
navigating with an American-made compass
That pimp of an instrument
whose hand always slaps toward gold

We are free and far from starving
We have spent our existence
preparing beauty after beauty
We have fed more souls
than we will ever know

It is impossible to dream bigger than this
What more could I ask of the Lord
when God has
filled us with art
Graced me with you

RainyMood.Com

It's 90 degrees and sunny outside. I'm peering through the window of a café, listening to a thunderstorm on loop. I love a good downpour. I never understood why so many people despise the rain. In the desert I was raised, precipitation is divine grace. A holiday. A reason to make a half-naked, puddle-stompin' fool of oneself. You're easily embarrassed. Overly mindful. Always sorry... sorry. You call it polite. I call it Canadian guilt. I'm painfully American. Black and unapologetic. I refuse to feel shame for any joy. Screeching laughter. Earthquake bass. Frolicking in God's gifts. Like that one time we took our 20-something-selves to Signal Hill in our bathing suits. The flash flood turned the child's playground into a water-park. We zoomed down the winding-river-slide again and again. Not sorry. Not sorry at all when children and their parents appeared. But we did walk home. Slowly... slowly. Trying not to slip on the beauty falling all around us, flooding beneath us. How deep are these roots? Will this storm lead to a generous bloom, or mudslide our sapling away? When the natural disaster ran its course. When the skies calmed with sadness, you moved back to your country. You said we see life too different. You love a good heat-wave. You sit in coffee shops in Vancouver, peering through glass at the 9 to 5 rain. Praying it takes a vacation. Dreaming of southern California sun. Both of us wondering; what went wrong?

Expiration Date

My date asks about the women you drew
All three keeping watch on my bedroom walls

I am relieved for the chance to praise you
To explain why I am not worth her time
How this heart was on the clearance rack
This night an expiration date already passed
This love spoiled before it is even open

I explain how the portraits are **not** photographs
but penciled by the impossible hands
of a woman who can see every wrinkle in my soul
A woman who can capture me in ways
no one else ever will
A woman so filled with holy
It is hard to tell the difference
between her touch and God's

Quantum Physical Faith

In a parallel universe
God the Mother

has a prodigal daughter who is
welcomed home with a feast

In a parallel universe
we eat each other

up and down
A holy communion

A shameless sacrament
necessary for salvation

In a parallel universe
we share

the same faith
instead of the same doubt

In this universe
we stare

through the same rainbow-
stained glass window

Me looking out
You looking in

Both
wondering

if we are on the proper
side of these church walls

Catching the dying belief
in each other's eyes

Somehow
this keeps both our faith alive

Micah Bournes

PROPHESIES

Micah Bournes

Where It Will Come From

Something tiny
So small I can smuggle
it in my pocket
but I don't

Pockets and sleeves
are too obvious
People expect
wealth and magic
to come from them
even when empty
Especially when empty

The barren fridge I keep opening
Fully aware of its famine
Still searching its shelves for
something tiny

Something simple
Hidden in the last place
I would think to hide things
Not hidden at all
Overlooked
Faithful in its forgottenness
Still there when I return from
chasing each mirage
It has always been
something tiny

A million tiny things
Ant-like
parading across
my unkept hope
Each one
carrying joy
well beyond its weight

Gospel

Halfway through my first
acceptance letter
the spirit
A spirit
Several spirits
(all of them holy)
unbroke my wildness
Colonized limbs
began to move with
freedom of Africans
who lived and died without
ever seeing a white man

I don't even dance
Got a finger snap of butt cheeks
Yet I explode from the desk
Find myself
in the hallway
twerkin' on ghosts

There is nothing sexy
or shameful
about my booty shakin'
I feel the fire
The ancestors encircled
in celebration

Every preacher I know
has told me the word
Gospel
means good news
I wonder why
a sermon has never
made me twerk

This
is how God
is meant to move a soul

Prunus Persica

At 8 years old I became a botanist. In the backyard of our new home stood a modest tree. My parents claimed it was a peach tree, but all I saw was flowers. My skepticism drove me to observe the specimen close. How exactly these pink and white petals would magically transform into fuzzy balls of food was beyond me. But I was determined not to blink. The flowers died slowly as the peaches began to form. The tree's stature was deceitful. Small and cute, I hypothesized it might produce a basket full, at best, until the branches began to break, so heavy with plenty. The peaches ripened in waves. The first taste erased all traces of atheism from my scientific mind. The fruit was candy-sweet. The tree was a grocery-store-gum-ball-machine in my backyard and you didn't even have to put a quarter in. My mother loved homegrown fruit. That tree was her dream come true. My father loved free food. That tree was his excuse to never purchase groceries again. It was bliss . . . for a week. In those seven days I ate more peaches than I had in my first eight years of life. The thrill was gone, but the peaches, were not. Piles of over-ripened fruit rotted beneath the tree. In the name of starving children in Africa, my father refused to buy any other food.

"Dad, we're out of cereal."
        "Eat a peach."
"Dad we have bread but no meat."
        "Eat a peach."
"Dad, mom's sick, she didn't make dinner."
        "Eat a peach."
"Dad, I'm still hungry."
        "Eat another peach."

This tyranny drove me and my five siblings back to science as we began to experiment the culinary possibilities for Prunus Persica. Modern day George Washington Carvers, we would not rest at peach pie and peach cobbler. We concocted peach cookies, peach smoothies, peach juice, peach syrup, peach pancakes, peach sandwiches, peach burritos, peaches and yogurt, peaches and ice cream, peach salad, sautéed peaches, fried peaches, baked peaches, we gave peaches away by the bowlful and still were plagued with baskets more! *How long, oh Lord, must we eat this manna?* How quickly had we forgotten the wonder. Complaining over what we once gave thanks. Unimpressed, with what we used to consider miraculous.

Drake Park Revival

The women sang familiar melodies
with unfamiliar speech
The preacher stood at the cross-
roads of 10th and Maine
proclaiming Jesus Cristo

I cannot repent in Spanish
so he handed me a flyer (in Spanish)
and left me alone

I walked home unsure
if his gospel was
good news for the poor
or gays go to hell

I prayed to Black Jesus
that these spiritual siblings of mine
do no harm to my neighbors

I pretend like I would say something
if I understood the sermon
and it *was* harm

Across from the park
an apartment window
displays a homemade poster
in English
Bold ink
It reads

CLOSE THE CAMPS

without hesitation
my spirit shouts

PREACH

Ten Thousand Cranes

Thrice useless
The origami crane is
bird without flight
Paper which cannot be written upon
A magicless charm

As legend is told
The hands that fold
one thousand cranes are granted
a wish of healing and peace
I look up and see ten thousand

The strings of fragile
birds descend from high ceilings
in the infusion center
More specifically
The Todd Cancer Pavilion

I do not have cancer
but my ailment is fierce enough
to need cancer-strength drugs
Superstition
Divine intervention

The cranes collect dust
stuck halfway to heaven
as fortunes worth of
bronze penny prayers turn green
at the bottom of lifeless fountains

I ran into Amy Azaren from 5th grade
She was here to comfort
her diseased mother
The old woman never
saw another Hanukkah

Amy noticed I was alone
at the cancer pavilion
Chased off her fears with a smile
She could not hold another grief
She could not fold another thousand

Do not worry friend
I will be here
for several Christmases
There are enough cranes already
None of them are working

There are enough gods already
None of them are healing
And yet we keep hoping
Fingers folding prayers
we've little faith will fly

None of this is offensive to me
Death is not as hideous as hopelessness
I look up and see ten thousand cranes
It is the greatest beauty
I witness all day

Can You Repeat The Question?

A list of things I'm afraid of in no particular order:

-Dance floors
        Not dancing
        Dance floors
        Dancing in public

-I'm afraid of loving the poems more than the muse
        Of making poor art
        Of being obsessed with making good art
        Forgetting why I make art in the first place

-I'm afraid of being a bad husband one day
        Of putting my work before my bride
        Having a wandering eye
        A sharp tongue
        Becoming a lazy romantic
        Being arrogant

-I'm afraid of how much I love being right

-I'm afraid of being wrong
        Being wrong about God
        Dying and decomposing into nonexistence
        Into whatever I was before birth
        Of praying to Jesus
        then crossing into eternity
        to tremble before the throne of
        a truth I never knew
        A love I never worshipped
        When my faith is doubtful
        I fear that I've been blowing hot air for years
        Calling people to believe in false hope
        I know there's no way the scientific method
        can guarantee the most important facts

-I'm afraid 'cause I know I have to believe
      Have to wait
      Have to live by faith

-I'm afraid of racist dogs with sharp teeth
      and their owners who swear they're harmless
      Who swear they usually never act like this
      Who don't know what's gotten into them
      or where they got it from

-I'm afraid of my blind spots
      Of not smellin' my own stank when
      others felt the funk a mile away

-I'm afraid of easy answers
      Of solutions that seem too convenient
      When the truth always aligns with my perspectives
      I have to question the way I measure truth

-I'm afraid of the day I stop asking questions
      When I'm always the teacher and never the disciple
      I'm afraid of how difficult it is for me
      to be in the audience and enjoy the show
      To sit in the pew without being overly critical
      I'm afraid of the way I only love my own songs
      and trust my own thoughts

-I'm afraid I might be creating my own God

-I'm afraid I'll never know love 'cause I got too much fear
      And I've made it too comfortable
      I've catered to its every need
      I've let fear rest in the bed I made for love
      Gave it a foot-rub and cooked it breakfast
      Then got the nerve to wonder why love never comes
      my way
      I gotta take a shower and clean these sheets
      I'm afraid if love came
      they would smell the fear all over me
      But I'm afraid this fear won't leave until love busts
      down the door
      and I ain't heard a knock in years

-I'm afraid of metaphors
      Of being too poetic
      Of my message getting lost in imagery
      So I keep it straightforward and blunt

-I'm afraid of being too blunt
      Of not being poetic enough

-I'm afraid of not being respected by my poetry peers
      Of poets finding out that I don't know jack about
      poetry
      I don't know jack about Kerouac, Dickinson or
      Angelou
      I never studied the classics
      Didn't major in creative writing
      Never messed wit iambic pentameter
      Never read poetry books
      I'm afraid of how good I've gotten at frontin'

-I'm afraid of being the only black person on a panel
discussion
      I'm afraid of being seen as an expert on everything
      Just 'cause I talk good and write rhymes
      This fool has 3 Doctorates
      Homegirl has 4
      What am I here for?
      How did I get here?
      What am I doing?
      I'm afraid I don't know
      I'm sorry
      Can you repeat the question?
      Okay
      I'm sorry
      I'm afraid I don't know the answer

- I'm afraid I don't have the answers

Perfection

The man was given a beautiful plant. Every day he watered it with eagerness. Placing it precisely adjacent the window. Convinced that this position provided the perfect portion of solar sustenance. He took pride in his plant. He knew by the lushness of the leaves and the healthy bark that his labor of love was paying off. Until one morning he poured delicately into the pot, and water spilled over. He looked closer and saw the plant was flooded. It wasn't absorbing the drink. His love had been sitting stagnant. Confused, he rubbed his fingers against the leaves... plastic. Perfect. Unreal. His heart drowned as he despised the same perfection in which he once took pride. The plant's beauty was repulsive. A thief. Stealing affection intended for something that could actually receive love. Something less than perfect. Something that could die. Something worth mourning. Something   .   .   .

Alive.

Fingerprints

A slender Catholic candle
The kind you use to worship God
or remember someone murdered in the street
This one is blank
Saintless
Gold ring around the brim
Off-white flesh
The scent reads
Perfume
The wick burns
slow
The flame
humble
The aroma
familiar
It smells of faint smoke and newborn child
Hot milk boiling with sugar
Rushing river
Fresh laundry
So subtle you might mistake it for clean air
A mountaintop breath of serenity in this smoggy ghetto
The tiny light puddles my eloquently waxed despair
It is not the solid thing I knew it to be
I touch the warm moat surrounding the flame
Let the lava mold to the grooves of
fingerprints the earth has never seen
Remember I am wonderfully made
Wonder what I was afraid of in the first place
Slowly peel away lies clinging to my skin

Stages Of Inhumanity

At 4 to 5 weeks:

The (not a human) heart begins to form
Along with the (not a human) brain and spinal cord
(not a human) Arm and leg buds appear
Your (not a human) baby is now
an embryo and one-twenty-fifth inch long

At 8 weeks:

Your (not a human) baby's heart beats with a regular rhythm
The (not a human) arms and legs grow longer
(not a human) Fingers and toes have begun to form
The (not a human) sex organs begin to form
The (not a human) eyes have moved forward on the
(not a human) face
At the end of eight weeks
Your (not a human) baby is a fetus and
looks more like a human (but is not a human)

At 16 weeks:

(not a human) Muscle tissue and bone continue to form
creating a more complete (not a human) skeleton
(not a human) Skin begins to form
Your baby makes sucking motions with the (not a human) mouth

At 20 weeks:

(not a human) Eyebrows eyelashes fingernails
and toenails have formed
Your (not a human) baby can even scratch itself
Your (not a human) baby can hear and swallow

At 24 weeks:

(not a human) Bone marrow begins to make
(not a human) blood cells
Taste buds form on your baby's
(not a human) tongue
(not a human) Footprints and fingerprints have formed
Real (not a human) hair begins to grow on your baby's
(not a human) head

At 32 weeks:

Your baby's (not a human) bones are fully formed
Your baby's (not a human) kicks and jabs are forceful
The (not a human) eyes can open and close and sense
changes in light
Lungs are not fully formed
but practice breathing movements (for not a human breath)

Weeks 37-40:

At 39 weeks your baby is considered full-term (not a
human)
Your baby's organs are ready to function on their own
As you near your due date
your baby may turn into a head-down position for birth

(Fully prepared to enter this upside down earth)

*Informational text taken from the U.S. Department of
Health and Human Services: WomensHealth.Gov*

Monsters

The Octagon Apartment Complex
on Roosevelt Island used to be
The Metropolitan Hospital
These eight walls were
meant to contain the contagious
Help the dying die in peace
The openly wounded scab over and scar closed
The first time mothers scream out
a screaming life

The Metropolitan Hospital
on Roosevelt Island used to be
The New York City Lunatic Asylum
These eight walls have been
prison for the seers of invisible
The hearers of God
Prophetic throats that shattered
palace windows from outside the gate
Shrieking into the dismissive void

And now
with ghosts of the crazy and
the sickly and the terrified new
these eight walls get to be called home
Luxury apartments full of mentally stable
physically capable professional human beings
A house is only haunted by the souls
we refuse to invite inside
By the shrills of the bleeding we pretend to not hear
By the yells we confine to sound-proof rooms

Some believe this building
has been redeemed
But for the first time
these eight walls
may be filled
cell to cell to cell
with the fiercest of monsters

Mouthfuls Of God

Fried hard or scrambled with cheese
I used to think sunny side up was a sin
Along with sushi and rare beef
Actual sins

Morally wrong
Gateways to cannibalism
Convinced by some
Old Testament verse about blood

And how Momma prepared
everything with flames of caution
Disgusted by meat still pink with death
Yolk runny with life

The way my mother
does anything
is not a matter of taste
but righteousness

I am still learning
to unvirgin my bless-ed Mary
That her opinions are
not infallible scripture

I am still learning
to dismiss the shame I feel when
consuming certain joys
Not every appetite is Eve's rebellion

So much of life is holy
Mouthfuls of God
I swallow flesh and blood
with gratitude

I thank the Lord for
freedom's sweetness
instead of groveling
for forgiveness

Micah Bournes

Almost Love

It was not the first time
a white pastor told me
my message was true
but his congregation was not ready
That he nearly lost his pulpit
after letting me speak
That he agrees with every word
but cannot keep pressing
with such urgency
That I must be gentle with hatred
That privilege is addictive
A drug to be weaned off gradually
Four centuries and counting
That half his church left
after hearing good news for the poor
And what good is preaching
if there is no one in the pews
No tithes in the bucket
Surely I must understand how
a man needs to feed his family
How the sacrifice would be too great
How it pains him to even admit this
How it almost feels like a bullet to the chest
Almost feels like a noose to the neck
Almost feels like a nail to the wrist

Almost

Spaghetti Revolution

When he realized
I was trying to rhyme the world free
the man at the post office
likened poetry to spaghetti
Suggested them both
powerless in the face of real danger

> *What's poetry gonna do*
> *if someone run up in here*
> *with a gun?*

I tried to explain
He talked over my answer
I stopped trying to explain
Kept packing poetry books
like bombs
Kept serving poems
like Italian grandmothers
murdering the ache of everyone
with hunger in their eyes

Micah Bournes

Here Comes This Dreamer

They saw him from afar, and before he came near to them they conspired against him to kill him. They said to one another, "Here comes this dreamer. Come now, let us kill him and throw him into one of the pits."
— Genesis 37:18-20

Here comes this dreamer

they whispered
Meaning to insult
What a lovely way
to show disdain

Here comes this dreamer

said the brothers
Said the enemies
Said the dreamless that
wanted his vision

He was favored
He was young
He was gifted
But they were most offended
by his dream
They tried to kill the prophet
in hopes of killing the prophecy

Here comes this dreamer

said the sightless with murder in their eyes
But you cannot kill what you cannot see
You cannot silence a voice you cannot hear
You cannot disbelieve in dreams
that were never yours

Poquito Más

There is little room for want
when I eat a shrimp burrito for dinner
When a friend and I harmonize
to love songs we wrote together
When home is a house full of artists
Walls full of canvas
When my bookshelves are bursting with spines
When there are nutrients for my hungry mind
When I fight for my right to live
and live
When my sickness is not yet unto death
When the beauty I began to doubt is revealed
When the poem finally arrives in the 23rd hour
When dreams fill my days with good sweat
My nights with good rest
When my bedroom walls sing the blues with black pride
When my room transforms into a habitat
A haven
When a haven is only as peaceful as
the soul that dwells in it
When my soul creates calm instead of longing for it
When my still waters are stirred by the life they invite
When tomorrow makes no promises
When that mystery makes me smile
When the unknown
is more adventure than anxiety
When there is ample reason to complain
but I save this breath for bellowing joy
When perspectives shift
When gratitude becomes discipline
When discipline creates more freedom than
refusing to commit
When commitment feels less like a leash
More like love
When love feels more like it exists

When existence is more gift than crisis
When life is a work of art
When I trust there is an author
When I trust in the author
and the story being written
is not lacking a thing
When my cup runneth over
but my table is never full
When my heart always has room
for a little more

Freakshow

       Never dismiss the visions of
Madmen
       Wisdom can be gathered from
       anyone who sees what
       others cannot
Drunk men
       tell no tales
Poets
       cannot lie
Poets
       cannot lie because
       we do not divide fact from fiction
       There's often more truth in our
       fantasy worlds and metaphors
       than human courts where
Liars
       swear to speak honestly in
       the name of laws they break
       In the name of gods they disobey
       The prayers of
The Proud
       will never reach heaven
       But
God
       hears the slurred words of the
Stumbling Prophets
       And all will be cursed who
       mock them
       It is not an easy task to
       plead with the world
       To grieve for the world
       Especially since
God
       often speaks through
       those most-broken

The picture we paint in our
minds is a far cry from the
reality of heaven
When
The Saints
    go marching in
    it will not be a parade of
    the almost perfect
God
    does not reserve grace
    for those who only need
    a little bit
The Healthy
    are in no need of a doctor
The Healer
    is for
The Sick
    Heaven will be a freakshow
Promiscuous Young Men
    will embrace the
Virgin Priests
    who molested them
    and their hearts
    will both be pure
    How amazing
    is grace
The Street-Corner Preacher
    will be greeted by
    thousands of people
    she thought were not listening
    Thank you for enduring the
    times we mocked you
    Your sidewalk sermons
    are why we know
God

How amazing
is grace
Aborted Children
will tug the spotless robes of
Young Women
and say
Hello mother
I'm so glad to finally meet you

The Former Master
will see the lashed back of
His No-Longer Slave
and say
You taught me the love of
The Savior
The Suicide Bomber
who prayed for forgiveness
during the millisecond
between pressing the detonator
and standing before
the throne of
God
The Guilty Thief
hanging next to
Jesus
on the cross
The Madman
who spoke to invisible beings
will stand between
Michael
and
Gabriel
with a grin as wide as
an angel's wingspan and scream
I KNEW I WASN'T CRAZY!

The Mrs.
      and
The Mistress
The Victim
      and
The Rapist
The Foreign
      and
The Racist
The Bullies
      and
The Geeks
      All those who somewhere
      along the way believed
      Whose sins were forgiven
      and strength was given
      to love
      their
Enemies
      So many we swore
      there is no way in hell
      we would see them in heaven
      But they will be there
      We will be there
      with a song on our lips
      and our eyes full of faith
      and we'll sing
      How amazing is
Grace

Afterword

I hesitate to call myself a dreamer. I undoubtedly am one, I just don't like the stereotypes. We're seen as overly optimistic do-gooders with fantasies of utopia. Stubborn, starving artists, desperate for an ever elusive big break. Hippies and non conformists avoiding stable employment for no apparent reason. Whatever type of dreamer you're damned to be, the greatest misconception about us is that we're disconnected from reality. Society tells us our heads are in the clouds. For me, this is the most isolating, most frustrating part about seeing the world as we do. The world, after all, was flat. Dreamers believed it round. The moon was unreachably far and devoid of air. Dreamers believed we could walk on it. Women were less than capable, Blacks were less than human. Dreamers fought for suffrage and abolition of slavery. Dreamers were persecuted by the Church, assassinated by the State, ostracized by society for believing blasphemous, impossible things. Things that are now widely accepted as common knowledge, objective truth. In the end, dreamers are the closest to reality, the most in tune with what is real. Despite this, when a dreamer challenges anything widely believed by their village, their nation, their generation, they become a threat, a disruption to the way things are. Dreamers are particularly threatening to those who possess power in the established order of any society.

My mother has been hilariously unsupportive of much of my life's work. It has always confused me. I know we share many of the same convictions. I also know she has suffered greatly from the institutional inequalities I seek to dismantle. My battle cry is "Fight Evil With Poetry". Shouldn't that make a mother proud? Why is she such a dream-killer? One day, I was catching her up on the things I'd been creating and the issues they addressed. In a fretful exhaustion she exclaimed, "You already Black, now you gotta go and say all these things to make [white people] mad. Why can't you just leave it alone. It's like you're painting a target on your own back." It was in this moment that I finally understood my mother's resistance. She knows what this world does to dreamers. She knows how fragile and violent the egos of those with white privilege often are. As much as she cares about justice, she is a mother first, she only wants her son to be safe. I do not fault her for her sentiments, but after that conversation, I was able to release myself from the desire for her approval. I cannot put safety first, I cannot be quiet. Trust me, I've tried. I'm embracing everything that comes with being a dreamer. All the eyerolls, the laughter, the hate mail, the crosshairs on my back.

I chose the title "Here Comes This Dreamer" because I wanted to trick the reader. The name itself sounds quite romantic, a poetic cliché appropriate for one with his head in the clouds. I wanted to call to mind the dismissive, patronizingly affectionate stereotypes western culture has about dreamers. People think they admire us. However naïve and misguided they take us to be, many claim to consider dreamers noble and beautiful people. The truth is revealed when you arrive at the title poem in the collection. The reality is, like Joseph's brothers in Genesis 37, when society sees dreamers approaching, historically, the response has been, "Here comes this dreamer, come now, let us kill him and throw him into one of the pits".

Despite this danger, I must live by my convictions. I do not merely seek to reflect the world's pain in my art, but inject hope into dismal perspectives, to challenge the way humanity sees itself, the way America sees itself. I pray the things I create help wean people off their comfort addiction, clears the fog of greed, violence, and racism clouding the vision of so many Americans, opens eyes to the abundant beauty that already exists. I do not merely dream of what ought to be, of what is possible in an uncertain future, or a sinless afterlife. I dream with every step. I walk by faith, not by sight. I work and pray to help more and more humans learn to live in the divine now, on earth, as it is in heaven.

– Micah Bournes

About The Author

Micah Bournes is poet and musician from Long Beach, California. His work explores questions of culture, justice, and faith. In addition to performing, he often speaks and teaches workshops on creative writing, activism through art, and the way of Jesus. Discover more of his work at:

MicahBournes.com.

If you'd like to help Micah continue to Fight Evil With Poetry consider supporting him monthly at

Patreon.com/MicahBournes
Instagram: @MicahBournes
Email: contact@micahbournes.com

GRATEFUL

This book was created in community with my official Partners In Rhyme

Anne McCaslin

Brandon Piliavin

Toby and Amanda Mckeehan

Dave Taylor and Stephanie D'Costa

Nathan and Sharon Tsang-de Lyster

Bridgeway Christian Church of Roseville California

and the dozens of patrons who believe in my poetry and music

ANTHOLOGY

FIGHT EVIL WITH POETRY

VOLUME ONE

EDITED BY
MICAH BOURNES + CHRIS CAMBELL

Also Available from Sideshow Media Group

CPSIA information can be obtained
at www.ICGtesting.com
Printed in the USA
BVHW080747221020
591508BV00007B/149/J

9 781649 709127